LONDON YESTERDAY

Published by GINGKO PRESS Inc.
5768 Paradise Drive, Suite J, Corte Madera, CA 94925, USA
Phone (415) 924–9615, Fax (415) 924–9608
email Gingko@linex.com
Copyright© English Edition 1998

3–927258–68–7

"London Yesterday: Leben in den 20er und 30er Jahren"
First published 1996 by Kunstverlag Weingarten, Germany
Copyright© 1996 Kunstverlag Weingarten GmbH

← View over London

LONDON

YESTERDAY

Gingko Press
Corte Madera, California
1998

Big Ben seen from Westminster Bridge

INTRODUCTION

LONDON YESTERDAY is not just pure nostalgia!

It is a remarkable collection of photographs that provide us with fascinating glimpses of life in one of the world's greatest cities during the twenties and thirties. The images teach us lessons about life, about continuity and change, about the human and urban condition. These pictures, taken three generations ago, open a window to the past, and in doing so, shed light on the present. Whatever our own images of London may be, formed through either direct or indirect experience, we are forced to compare them with the pictures of yesterday, seeking either congruence or discrepancy. We encounter corroboration, irritation, even correction, and as a result we gain new insight.

One thing is plain to see: London has always been full of hustle and bustle - traffic problems and overcrowding are nothing new. It is, and always has been, a very lively place: amiable, exciting to live in and (relatively) safe. Back in the 30s one could move about undisturbed, even in the famous night life district of Soho (which got its name from the calls of the hunters who used to chase hare there when it was still a heath). Because entertainment establishments of the highest and lowest order could be found right next door to each other, Soho always attracted a 'healthy' melange of interesting visitors.

Of course, it was not only in Soho that the rich and the poor, the locals and the exotic mingled in the streets. London in the 1920s and 1930s was more than just a large city in an industrialised country – it was the hub of a powerful empire that spanned the globe. London brought people and goods together from every corner of the Earth, and fostered a worldly generosity that was visibly most predominant in its architecture and urban planning.

In contrast to its cosmopolitan character, however, London had another side - the resolute world of native Londoners whose close knit circles were virtually impossible to penetrate. To be considered Cockney, for example, the most "authentic native Londoner", one must be born within the sound of "Bow Bells", the church bells of St. Mary-Le-Bow. (This is the type of definition that is so typical of London in that it is both precise and blurred.)

A distinguished amiability emanates from many pictures of London, and the photos published within these pages are no exception. London is a unique combination of the near and the far, the native and the foreign, and it is shown here wearing many different faces.

A photograph is by nature a direct interpretation of reality, but this does not mean that photography is not artistic. The images that have been brought together in this collection are "only" press photographs and hardly any of the photographers would have considered himself an artist. Their initial purpose was simply to document history, but their aesthetic organisation and artistic character make them exciting and stimulating even 60 years later.

Press photographers have always been aware of how important a strong visual impact is for the printed page. Most know through experience that the most unusual subject is worthless if it is inadequately or unconvincingly portrayed. Conversely, a perfect photographic execution can turn a banal, everyday subject into a work of art.

LONDON YESTERDAY is a collection of greatly varied and touching social and human documents. It unveils a great deal of gentle humour in moving everyday scenes that have preserved their power far beyond their time - like the pigs being directed across Camden Way by a Bobby – honi soit who doesn't smile.

Gerhard Charles Rump

Fleet Street on a normal workday

Infra-red photograph showing London seen from the Shell-Mex Building

View of the Thames and Lambeth Bridge taken from the roof of the House of Parliament

↑ The so-called "pool" of London, where goods from big freighters were loaded to barges, Tower Bridge in the background

← View over the Thames to warehouses and St. Paul's

The "pool" of London with Tower Bridge in the background

↑ Building the new Waterloo Bridge 1938

← Loading wooden boards to horse-drawn carts, Lambeth Bridge and House of Parliament in the background

↑ Building site of the new Waterloo Bridge 1938   → A tug on the stormy Thames near Blackfriars

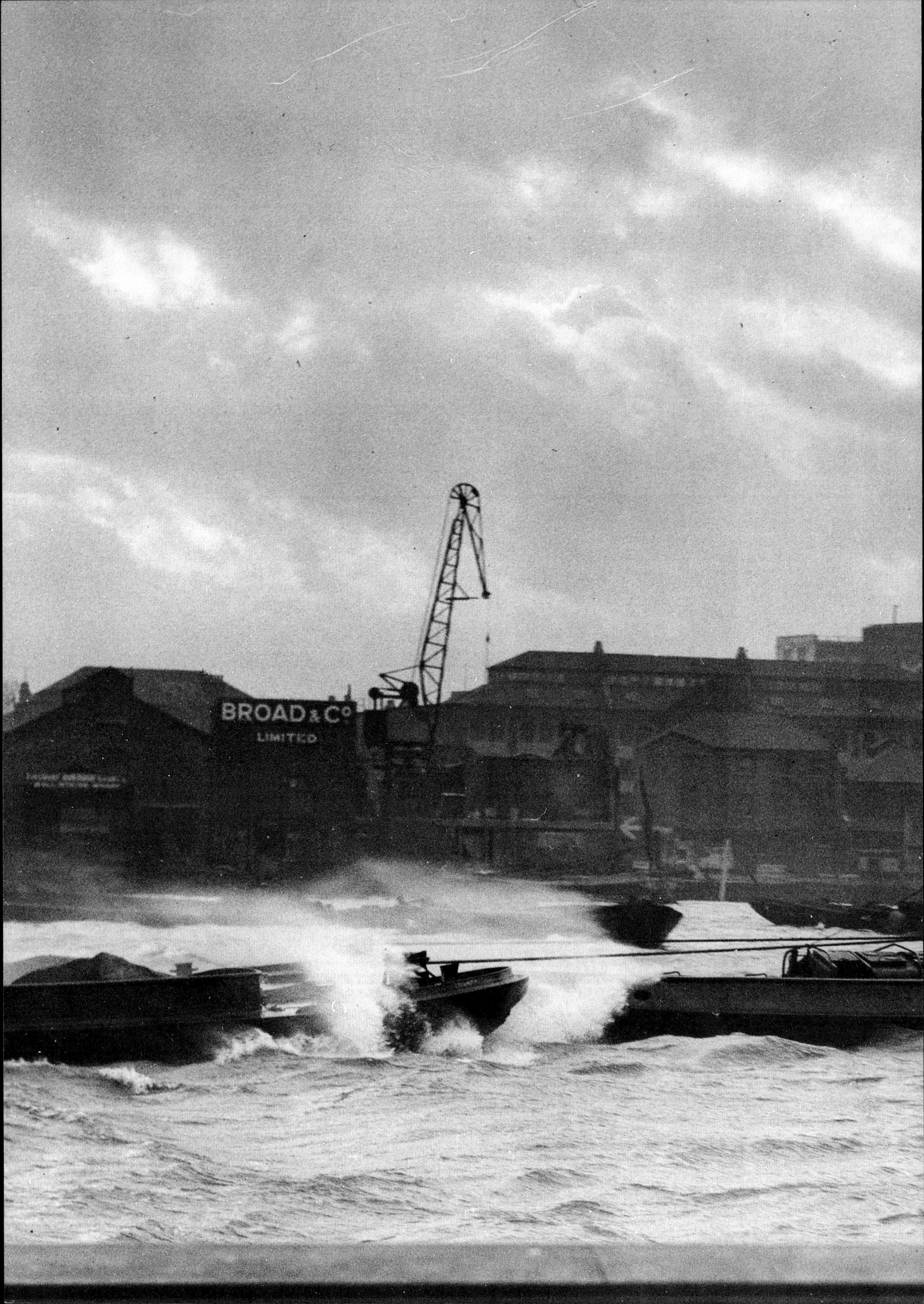
BROAD & Co
LIMITED

↑ The roof tops of London

→ Sir Alan Cobham's aircraft after take-off to Africa, November 17th, 1927

→ A wonderful view over the city of London seen from St. Paul's cupola (page 26/27)

↑ Hatton Garden and the monument to Prince Albert

← Piccadilly Circus at night

A newly erected building with luxury apartments near Baker Street Station (1932)

↑ Selfridge's department store in Oxford Street

→ The BBC's new radio building was nearing completion in 1935. Its unusual shape was chosen so that the lower flats on the right got enough daylight

For the opening of the "International Illumination Congress" on Ausgust 31st, 1931, some historic buildings were illuminated at night, like Tower Bridge (above) and Buckingham Palace (page 35)

The roof of the new Bank of England

A tourist attraction: the smallest house in England, closed in by two stately mansions on Bayswater Road.

↑ Playing and relaxing in London Parks →

← Sand-box in Victoria Gardens (next to the Houses of Parliament)

↑ Opening of the first children's pool in Hamsworth Park on Lambeth Road, July 1938

→ Margate Beach, August 1935

Fleet Street

↑ A luxury double-decker bus, with three axles, seating 62 people, used in London since the mid-thirties

→ Snowstorm near Westminster Bridge, March 9th, 1931

Traffic jam caused by snow in February 1932, Ludgate Circus

Completely overcrowded bus (of an independent company) during the General Strike of 1926

↑ Queuing in front of a newly opened station at Piccadilly Circus

← Traffic at Mansion House underground station (1932)

↑ Escalators in the new Piccadilly Circus station   → Charing Cross Underground station at night

↑ The "Silver Link", Great Britain's fastest train, starting from King's Cross station on September 30th, 1935 for its first journey

← People regularly flocked to weekend trains

Clothes market in Middlesex Street (Petticoat Lane)

↑ Christmas shoppers on Oxford Street   → Petticoat Lane Market a few days before Christmas 1936

On the way to the market

French onion merchant with onions from Brittany, sought-after in London

↑ Cleaning up after market

← Billingsgate Fish Market, then London's biggest and most important fish market in Lower Thames Street

Participants of a pony and donkey show in Regent's Park, organized by street merchants

Women peeling peas in Covent Garden

↑ Flower ladies at Piccadilly Circus

→ A herd of pigs crossing the Camden Road on its way to the market (1932)

Huge choice of turkeys for Christmas dinner on Leadenhill Market

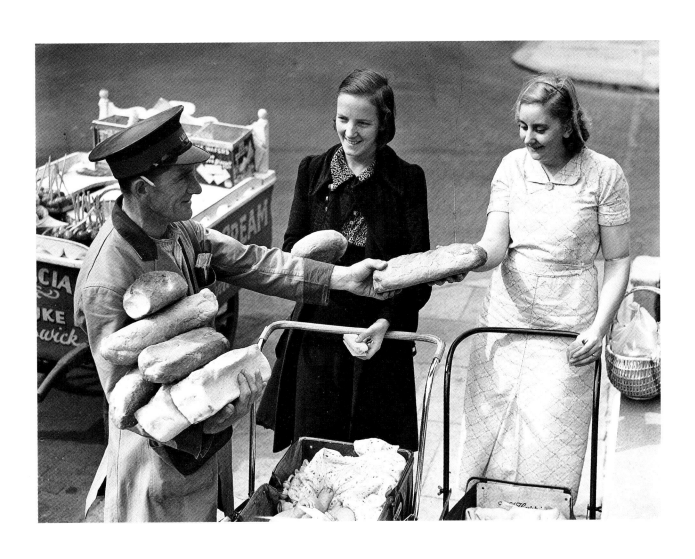

The price of bread was reduced by a half penny in August 1938

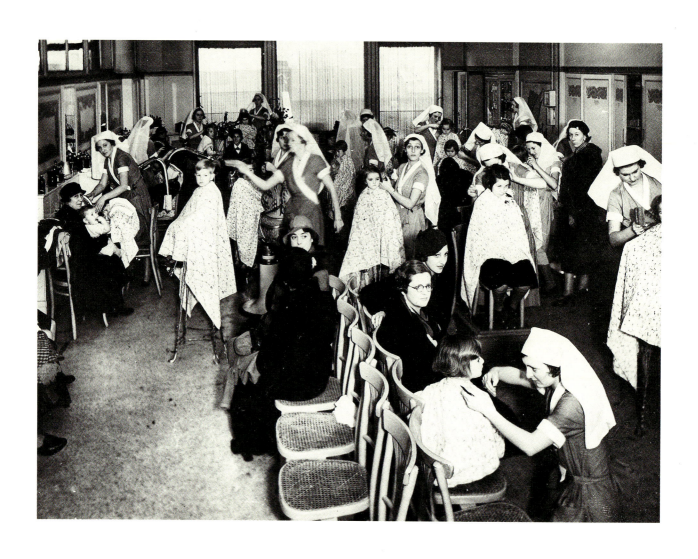

↑ "Bobba Shop", the childrens' hairdresser at Selfridge's

→ Sunlight bursting through the upper windows of Liverpool Street station

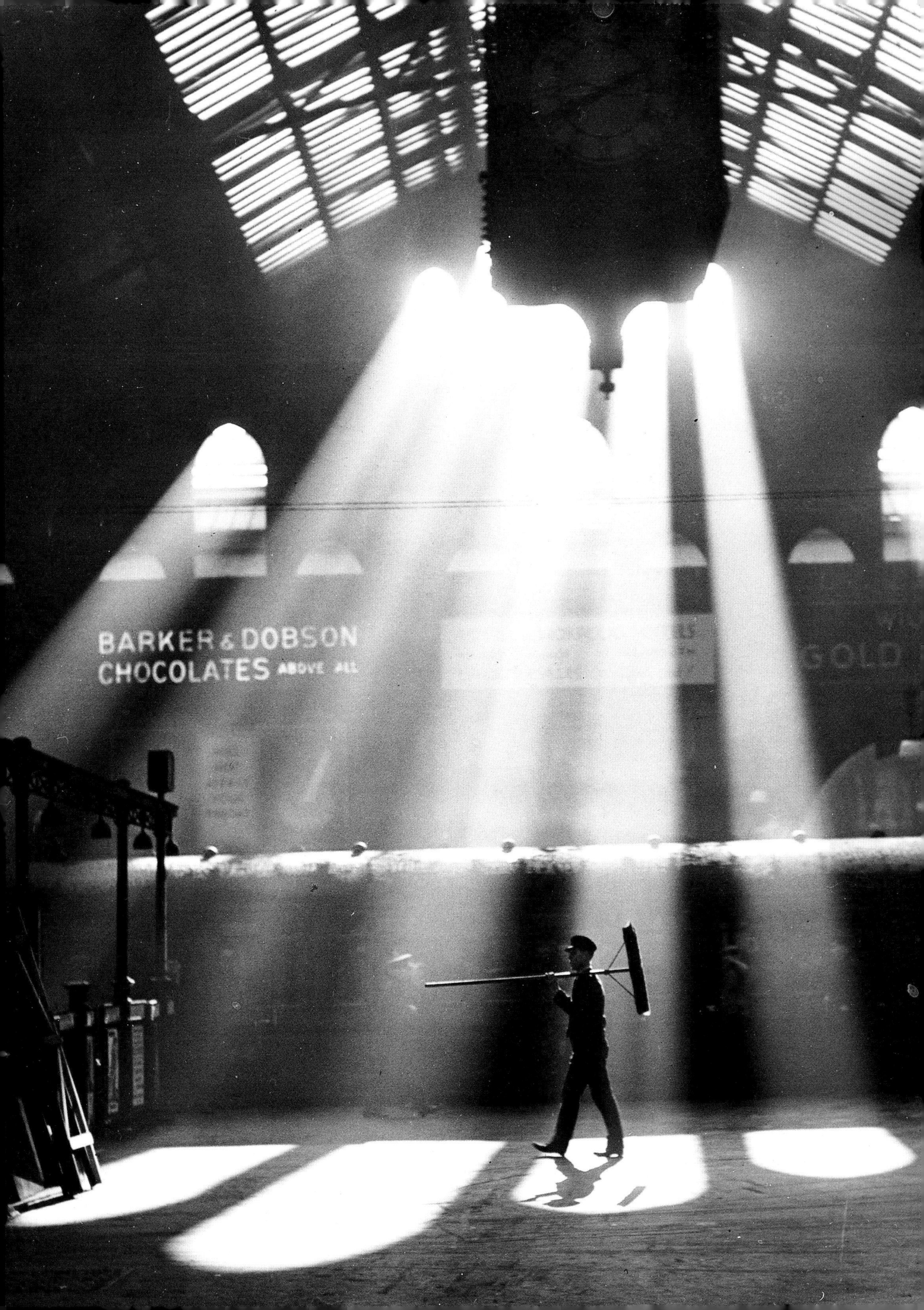
BARKER & DOBSON
CHOCOLATES ABOVE ALL

↑ Picket during the cotton weavers' strike in 1932

→ Building Lambeth Bridge in 1931

↑ Mother and child in Limehouse, East End

← Breakfast at Country Hall building site facing Big Ben

The "Rowe Sisters" dancers excited London with their shows (around 1927)

The opera season is open – a small part of the crowd queuing for tickets for hours

Traffic control in the autumn mist on the Mall, running through the Royal Gardens (1931)

King George V driving up in front of the Houses of Parliament for the opening of Parliament on October 28th, 1930

Workers erecting temporary grand stands for the mourning procession for George V in January 1936

A huge crowd bidding their last farewell to George V laying in state in front of Westminster Hall

↑ The queue of mourners at Westminster Hall was up to two miles long and more

→ Thousands withstand the pouring rain in order to witness the dress rehearsal of George VI's coronation

↑ Unusually dense traffic on George VI's Coronation Day (May 11th 1937)

← A merry crowd awaiting the coronation procession of Georgr VI

The royal coach on its way to Westminster Abbey

Cover Photo (front)   Building Lambeth Bridge in 1931
Cover Photo (back)   Completely overcrowded bus during the General Strike of 1926

All Photographs   Courtesy of:
                     THE INTERNATIONAL HISTORICAL PRESS PHOTO COLLECTION
                     of SWERIGES TELEVISION AB, Stockholm

Introduction   Gerhard Charles Rump

Translation   from the German language by
                     Donna Wiemann

Reproductions   Repro-Team GmbH, Weingarten
Printing and Binding Druck- und Verlagshaus Erfurt seit 1948, GmbH, Erfurt
Cover Design   Julie von der Ropp

Printed in Germany